seafood

First published in 2012 by
New Holland Publishers
London • Sydney • Cape Town • Auckland
www.newhollandpublishers.com

Garfield House 86–88 Edgware Road London W2 2EA United Kingdom
1/66 Gibbes Street Chatswood NSW 2067 Australia
Wembley Square First Floor Solan Road Gardens Cape Town 8001 South Africa
218 Lake Road Northcote Auckland New Zealand

A catalogue record of this book is available at the British Library and the National Library of Australia.

ISBN: 9781742573489

Publisher: Fiona Schultz
Publishing director: Lliane Clarke
Design: Keisha Galbraith
Production director: Olga Dementiev
Printer: Toppan Leefung Printing Limited

10 9 8 7 6 5 4 3 2 1

Follow New Holland Publishers on
Facebook: www.facebook.com/NewHollandPublishers

contents

Introduction

Seafood offers flavours to complement every occasion, from a casual barbecue to a formal dinner, and everything in between. In addition to offering a wealth of flavours, seafood is affordable, easy to prepare and endows a wide range of health benefits on those who eat it.

The world's oceans and inland waterways boast thousands of seafood species, and more than 300 of those are harvested commercially and caught by recreational fishers. We are also increasingly conscious of the importance of sustainable fishing and the protection of endangered species.

Seafood is an integral part of our lifestyle. Whether we are enjoying a sizzling summer's day, or in the middle of a snow storm in winter, we can choose a seafood dish to compliment the occasion.

This book offers traditional European recipes as well as Asian and modern North American dishes. It breaks down many of the perceived barriers people have about cooking with seafood.

The recipes are simple and easy to read and show that any type of seafood can be prepared easily for cooking. Because these recipes incorporate seafood they are not only wonderfully tasty but also very healthy.

Seafood is an important element in a well-balanced diet. Seafood is particularly good for those on low-fat diets.

Research shows that eating fish two or three times a week is a sure recipe for a healthy lifestyle. The small amount of fat in fish is rich in omega-3 fatty acids, making fish a great heart food, as it helps to keep your arteries healthy.

Recent studies show that eating seafood can even help those with rheumatoid arthritis, and that it reduces the risk of asthma in children.

Seafood is good news for slimmers. All seafood is low in kilojoules, with fewer kilojoules than even the leanest meat or chicken, and of course you will not have to trim any fat. Just grill, broil, barbecue, bake, steam or poach seafood to keep a low kilojoule count.

Seafood is an excellent source of top-quality protein and minerals, including iodine, zinc, potassium and phosphorus. It is also rich in vitamins, especially the B group.

Buying and Storing Fish

When buying fish, make sure it is fresh, and if you plan to freeze it, don't buy fish that has already been frozen. There are a few things to look for to tell if fish is fresh:

• It should not have a strong odour. Instead it should have a pleasant and mild 'sea' smell.
• The flesh should be firm with a smooth, slippery skin and no yellow discolouration.
• Whole fish should have bright eyes and red gills.

If you are worried about children swallowing bones, look for the many cuts available without bones. Try flake (also boneless hake), swordfish, marlin, tuna, blue grenadier, sea perch, salmon, John Dory, tail-pieces of ocean trout, ling and blue-eye cod. You will also find that many fish mongers now sell de-boned fillets such as salmon and trout.

If the fish has been packed in a plastic bag, unwrap it as soon as you get home and place it in a glass or stainless steel dish. Cover lightly with a damp tea towel and keep in the coolest part of the refrigerator. Use as soon as possible, and if not using the next day, place over a pan of ice.

If freezing, wrap fillets individually in cling wrap for easy separation. Always defrost in the refrigerator or microwave, or cook from frozen. Never thaw at room temperature, and never refreeze thawed fish.

Preparing fish

The two types of fish discussed here are described as flatfish(for example, flounder or sole) and round fish (for example, snapper or cod). Both types need to be cleaned before use, but cleaning procedures vary.

SCALING AND FINNING

Most fish will need to be scaled. However, there are a few exceptions, such as trout, tuna, shark, leatherjacket and others. When poaching a whole unboned fish, it is best to leave the dorsal and anal fins attached. This will help to hold the fish together during cooking.

Wash fish and leave wet, as a wet fish is easier to scale. Remove scales using a knife or scaler, starting at the tail and scraping towards the head (1).

Clip the dorsal fin with scissors or, if desired, remove both the dorsal and anal fins by cutting along the side of the fin with a sharp knife. Then pull the fin towards the head to remove it (2).

GUTTING

Gutting techniques are different for round fish and flatfish. When preparing fish to bone or fillet, remove the entrails by gutting through the belly. If you wish to serve the fish whole, preserve the shape of the fish by gutting through the gills.

• Round Fish

For boning or filleting, cut off the head behind the gill opening. Use a sharp knife and cut open the belly from head to just above anal fin (3). Remove membranes, veins and viscera. Rinse thoroughly.

To preserve shape of round fish, cut through the gills (4) and open outer gill with the thumb. Put a finger into the gill and snag the inner gill. Gently pull to remove inner gill and viscera. Rinse well.

• **Flatfish**

To gut, make a small cut behind gills and pull out viscera (5).

SKINNING

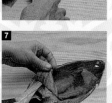

The tasty skin of some fish enhances the flavour. However, other fish have strong or inedible skin that interferes with the flavour. Always leave skin on when poaching or grilling a whole fish.

• **Round fish**

When skinning a whole round fish, make a slit across the body behind the gills, with another just above the tail. Then make another cut down the back (6).

Using a sharp knife, start at the tail and separate the skin from the flesh. Pull the knife towards the head, while holding the skin firmly with the other hand—do not use a sawing motion.

• **Flatfish**

to skin a whole flatfish, first turn the dark side up, then cut across the skin where the tail joins the body (7). With a sharp knife, peel the skin back towards the head until you have enough skin to hold with one hand (8).

Anchor the fish with one hand and pull the skin over the head. Turn fish over and hold the head while pulling the skin down to the tail.

CUTTING FILLETS

Fillets are pieces of boneless fish. There are slightly different techniques for filleting round fish and flatfish.

• **Round fish**

With a sharp knife, make a slit along the backbone from head to tail, then make a cut behind the gills.

Hold the head and insert the knife between fillet and ribs. Slide knife along the ribs (do not use a sawing motion), and cut down the length of the fish (9). Remove fillet by cutting off at the anal fin. Repeat on theother side of fish.

• **Flatfish**

Place skinned fish on chopping board with eyes up. Cut from head to tail through the flesh to the backbone, down the middle of the fish. Insert a sharp knife between the ribs and the end of the fillet near the head. Pull knife down the fillet on one side of the backbone and remove (10).

Cut off the remaining fillet in the same manner. Turn fish over and remove the two bottom fillets (11).

SKINNING A FILLET

Place fillet skin-side down and cut a small piece of flesh away from the skin close to the tail. Hold skin tight, and run a sharp knife along the skin without cutting it (12).

CUTTING A STEAK OR CUTLET

Using a solid, sharp chef's knife, cut off head just behind the gills. Slice the fish into steaks or cutlets of the desired thickness (13).

Preparing shellfish

A diverse and astonishing variety of shellfish is available for our cooking pot, including oysters, clams, mussels, crabs, prawns (shrimp), lobsters, squid and octopus. However, remember that out of water, shellfish deteriorate quickly.

OPENING BIVALVES

All bivalves—oysters, clams and mussels should be tightly closed when purchased. If you wish to use the shells in cooking, scrub them with a stiff brush under cold, running water.

• Oysters

If you use technique rather than strength, oysters are easy to open. Hold the unopened oyster in a garden glove or tea towel to protect your hand from the rough shell, and open the shell with an oyster knife held in the other hand.

Insert the tip of the oyster knife into the hinge (the pointed end), then twist to open the shell (14). Do not open oyster by attempting to insert the oyster knife into the front lip of the shell.

Slide the oyster knife inside the upper shell to cut the muscle that attaches oyster to the shell. To serve, discard the upper part of shell and cut muscle under bottom half, then replace oyster into half-shell (15).

• Clams

To open clams, use a blunt clam knife to avoid cutting the meat. Try freezing bivalves for half an hour to relax the muscles—they will be easier to open.

Slide blade of clam knife between two halves of shell. Work knife towards hinge until shell opens (16). Slide blade along

inside of one shell to cut muscles. Then do the same to other side to dislodge flesh (17).

• **Mussels**

The threads of tissue that protrude from the mussel shell are called the byssus or, more commonly, the beard. As mussels die quickly after debearding, prepare them immediately before cooking (18). Use the same technique for opening as for clams.

CLEANING CRABS

• **Hard-shelled crabs (mud crab)**

Wash and scrub under cold, running water. When clean, the entire crab may be poached or steamed. However, as most mud crabs are sold live, if you wish to cook the crab, you must first kill and disjoint it, then remove the edible parts.

To kill a crab instantly, stab just behind the eyes with the point of a sharp knife (19). Another killing technique is to place crab in freezer for a few hours.

Place crab on its back, and gently fold back tail flap or apron. Twist and pull off apron (20). You will find that the intestinal vein is attached and will pull out along with the apron. Discard.

Hold the crab with one hand where the apron was removed. Use the other hand to pry up the top shell. Tear-off and discard the top shell (21).

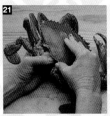

Remove the gills, take out the greyish sac and pull out mandibles from front of crab.

Hold the body where the legs are attached, and apply pressure so that crab splits in half along the centre of its body. Fold back halves and twist apart (22).

Twist off claws and legs where they join the body. Crack with hammer or nutcracker to make the meat easy to remove.

• **Soft-shelled crabs**

Cut across the eyes with a sharp knife. Pull out and discard the stomach sac. Turn over and lift the tail flap or apron and fold it away from the body. Pull out the apron and attached intestinal vein, and discard. Turn crab right-side up and lift flaps on each side near legs. Scrape off and discard spongy gills.

CLEANING PRAWNS (SHRIMP)

Most people prefer to remove the head and body shell before eating. However, the entire body of the prawn is edible, depending on the cooking method.

To peel, break off head, place finger on underside between legs, and roll prawn. The body shell will come away. Then squeeze tail section, and remainder of shell will slip off (23).

Slit down the middle of the outside curve to expose the intestinal vein. Remove it, and wash prawn under cold, running water (24). It is not necessary to remove the vein from bay or smaller prawns. However, veins of larger prawns sometimes contain shell or grit that can affect taste.

CLEANING YABBIES

Freshwater crayfish or yabbies can be found in many inland streams. They have very sweet meat in the tail. Usually they are cooked in their shells. To remove the intestinal vein, hold on a firm surface, right-side up (25).

Hold firmly with one hand and pull the tail flap away from the yabby to remove the intestinal vein (26).

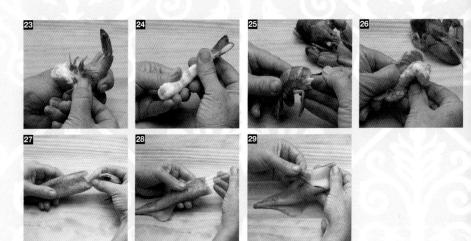

CLEANING SQUID

Squid can be poached, sautéed, fried, stuffed, baked and grilled, but do not overcook as it will become tough.

Rinse in cold water, and then cut off tentacles, just above the eye. Squeeze the thick centre part of the tentacles. This will push out the hard beak, which you should discard (27).

Squeeze the entrails out by running your fingers from the closed to the open end. Pull out the quill and discard (28).

Peel off skin by slipping finger under it. Pull off the edible fins from either side and also skin them (29).

OPENING ABALONE

Using a strong knife, force the blade tip into the thin part of the shell and underneath the flesh. Work blade backwards and forwards until muscle is freed from shell. Lift out flesh, remove intestine and wash flesh well under cold, running water.

Slice off dark heel (sucker pad). Slice the flesh horizontally in two, wrap slices in tea towel and pound well with the side of a meat mallet or cleaver until limp and velvety. Slices can be cut into thin strips or chopped, depending on cooking method.

CLEANING LOBSTER

You can purchase whole live or frozen lobster. Also available are uncooked frozen lobster tails and canned or frozen lobster meat.

To kill a live lobster, hold it on its back on a firm surface. With a heavy chef's knife, stab the point into the mouth to severe the spinal cord. You may also stun the lobster by placing it in the freezer for 30 minutes per 500g (17½oz).

Weigh to calculate cooking time. Place live lobster in a large pot of cold, salty water and bring to simmering point. Simmer, but do not boil, for 8 minutes per 500g (17½oz).

Hold lobster right-side up on a firm surface. Pierce the shell at the centre of the body behind the head (30).

Cut lobster in half lengthwise, and remove and discard sac near the head and intestinal vein in the tail (31). Remove any 'mustard' from the body and reserve for flavouring your sauces.

Clean the lobster by rinsing under cold, running water (32).

CLEANING OCTOPUS

Cut head from body section, just below the eyes, to remove tentacles. Cut out eyes and clean body cavity. Push beak up through centre of joined tentacles, cut off and dispose.

Wash thoroughly. Pay particular attention to tentacles as the suckers may contain sand.

Skin is difficult to remove from fresh octopus, but it may be left on for cooking. However, to remove skin, parboil in a little water for 5–10 minutes, then skin when cool enough to handle.

To clean a small, whole octopus, cut up back of head and remove gut. Push beak up and cut out. Cut out eyes and wash thoroughly.

The key to fresh fish

- Don't buy fish that has already been frozen.
- Fish should not have a strong odour—instead it should have a pleasant, sea smell.
- Whole fish should have bright eyes and red gills.
- The flesh should be firm, with slippery skin and no yellow discolouration.

shrimp & prawns

Chilli and Lemongrass Soup

serves 4

2 large tomatoes, each cut into
6 wedges

3 stalks lemongrass, sliced
diagonally into 4cm (1½in)
pieces

1½ tablespoons fish sauce, plus 1
tablespoon extra

8 kaffir lime leaves, torn into
quarters

1½ cups straw mushrooms

12 large raw prawns (shrimp),
shelled and deveined, tails
intact

1 red and 1 green bird's eye chilli,
crushed or left whole

juice of 3 limes

1 teaspoon sugar

¼ cup mint leaves

¼ cup coriander (cilantro) leaves

1 tablespoon naam phrik pao*
(Thai red chilli paste)

Heat 5 cups water in a wok or large pot until
nearly boiling. Add the tomatoes, lemongrass, fish
sauce, kaffir lime leaves and mushrooms. Bring
to the boil and allow to boil for 2 minutes. Stir and
add the prawns. Reduce heat to medium.

Gently push the prawns under the surface of
the broth but do not stir at this stage. After about
1 minute, or once the prawns are cooked, stir
gently.

Divide the chillies, soup, prawns and vegetables
between 4 large soup bowls. Season each bowl
with one quarter of the lime juice, sugar, mint,
coriander, extra fish sauce and naam phrik pao.

Stir each bowl gently, remove the lemongrass
and serve with steamed jasmine rice.

Note Naam phrik pao is available from Asian food
stores.

Marinated Shrimp in Bacon

serves 4

32 raw king prawns (shrimp), peeled and deveined

¼ cup fresh lime juice

1 clove garlic, crushed

4cm (1½in) piece fresh ginger, grated

2 tablespoons brown sugar

16 bacon strips, rind removed

Place prawns in a medium bowl with the lime juice, garlic, ginger and sugar and mix well. Cover and refrigerate for 30 minutes.

Cut bacon into strips about 2.5cm (1in) wide and wrap around each prawn. Thread two prawns onto wooden skewers.

Grill under a moderate heat for 2 minutes each side or until cooked through.

Char Koay Teow (Fried Noodles)

serves 4

2 teaspoons sambal oelek (chilli paste)

4 teaspoons kecap manis

4 teaspoons light soy sauce

4 teaspoons oyster sauce

300g (10½oz) thick, flat rice noodles

2 tablespoons vegetable oil

12 large raw prawns (shrimp), peeled

1 squid tube, cut into strips

4 cloves garlic, minced

4 eggs

1 large handful bean sprouts

100g (3½oz) clam meat

Cover the noodles with boiling water, leave for 15 minutes, then drain. Combine the chilli paste, kecap manis and sauces in a small bowl.

Heat a wok over medium-high heat and add the oil. Add the prawns and squid and stir-fry for about 10 seconds. Add the garlic and fry for another 10 seconds, stirring constantly.

Crack in the eggs and stir gently until just cooked. Add the noodles and stir briefly. Add the combined sauces.

Increase heat to high and stir-fry until the noodles are coated with sauce. Add the bean sprouts and clam meat and stir through.

Splash 4 tablespoons water in around the sides of the wok and stir-fry for about 15 seconds or until well combined but not too dry. Serve immediately.

Piri Piri-Spiced Shrimp

serves 4

1kg (2lb 3oz) medium raw prawns (shrimp)

1 tablespoon peanut oil

2 tablespoons lemon juice

2 teaspoons piri piri seasoning

2 teaspoons parsley flakes

1 clove garlic, freshly crushed

½ cup plain (all-purpose) flour

vegetable oil for deep-frying

Remove the heads and shells from the prawns, leaving the tails intact. Using a sharp knife, make an incision along the back of the prawn, remove the vein and cut into the prawn so it opens out.

Combine the peanut oil, lemon juice, piri piri seasoning, parsley and garlic in a bowl. Add the prawns and coat in the mixture. Dip the prawns lightly in the flour.

Heat the oil in a wok or frying pan. Cook the prawns in batches for 1–2 minutes or until golden and crisp.

Serve the prawns with lime wedges.

Seafood Rice with Chilli Lime Butter

serves 4

1 cup basmati rice

16 large raw prawns (shrimp)

2 teaspoons olive oil

100g (3½oz) butter, melted

1 red chilli, finely sliced

1 green chilli, finely sliced

1 small red onion, finely sliced

1 lime, peeled and cut into small dice

juice of 1 lime

½ cup fresh coriander (cilantro), chopped

Combine the rice with 2 cups water in a saucepan. Bring to the boil, reduce heat to low, cover and cook for 15 minutes, then allow to stand covered for 10 minutes.

Shell the prawns, leaving the tails intact. To butterfly the prawns, cut along the back, about halfway through. Remove the vein.

Heat the oil in a heavy-based frying pan, add the prawns and cook until they change colour and are just cooked through. Set aside and keep warm.

Return pan to heat, add butter, chillies and onion. Sauté for 1–2 minutes, then add cooked rice and chopped lime and mix well. Add prawns, season with lime juice, stir through coriander and serve.

Penang Mee

serves 4

heads and shells of 16 raw king
   prawns (shrimp), washed

1 teaspoon salt

16 raw king prawns (shrimp),
   shelled, tails intact

6 cups chicken stock

2 tablespoons peanut oil

6 French shallots, sliced

2 teaspoons sambal oelek (chilli
   paste)

200g (7oz) fresh egg noodles

2 handfuls bean sprouts

2 handfuls kangkung or Asian
   greens, sliced into 5cm (2in)
   pieces

2 boiled eggs, sliced

2 fish cakes, sliced

16 slices cooked pork (optional)

Place the prawn heads and shells in a pot with
2 cups water and the salt and bring to the boil.
When just boiling, add the prawns, reduce heat
and simmer for 4 minutes.

Remove the prawns and set aside. Meanwhile,
bring the chicken stock to the boil and reduce to
a simmer.

Strain the prawn stock into the chicken stock
and continue to simmer.

Heat a wok over medium heat and add the oil.
Add the shallots and fry until browned and crisp.

Add the sambal oelek and fry for about 3 minutes
or until aromatic, stirring constantly. Add the
contents of the wok to the stock with an extra
teaspoon salt.

Bring a large pot of water to the boil. Cook
noodles, bean sprouts and kangkung for about
30 seconds.

Drain and divide between 4 large soup bowls.
Top each with quarter of the boiled egg, fish cake,
pork and cooked prawns. Fill the bowls with
chicken stock mixture. Garnish with crispy fried
shallots.

Garlic Salad

serves 4

1 tablespoon extra virgin olive oil

4 cloves garlic, crushed

½ teaspoon chilli flakes

24 large raw prawns (shrimp),
   shelled and deveined

1 medium tomato, sliced

1 cos lettuce, outer leaves
   discarded

1 Lebanese cucumber, sliced into
   ribbons

salt and freshly ground black
   pepper

juice of 1 lime

juice of 1 lemon

Heat a large heavy-based frying pan, add the oil, garlic, chilli flakes and prawns. Cook, stirring constantly, until the prawns change colour, about 3 minutes.

Divide the tomato slices between 4 serving plates, top with lettuces leaves and cucumber ribbons. Add the prawns and pour over the pan juices. Season with salt and pepper, then squeeze over the lemon and lime juices and serve.

Sesame Coconut with Mango Salsa

serves 4

12 raw king prawns (shrimp),
    peeled, tails intact

salt and freshly ground black
    pepper

½ cup plain flour

1 egg, beaten

1 cup sesame seeds

1 cup desiccated coconut

2 tablespoons olive oil

50g (1¾oz) mixed salad leaves

MANGO SALSA

1 mango, peeled and finely diced

½ small red onion, finely diced

¼ cup coriander (cilantro),
    chopped

juice of 1 lime

salt and freshly ground black
    pepper

Butterfly prawns, then dust with salt, pepper and flour. Dip in egg, allowing the excess to run off, then dredge in a mixture of sesame seeds and coconut. Set aside.

To make salsa, mix the mango, onion, coriander and lime juice in a bowl and season to taste.

Heat the oil in a frying pan, add the prawns and fry over a high heat for 1–2 minutes each side until golden.

To serve, divide the salad leaves between each plate and top with 3 cooked prawns and a generous spoonful of mango salsa.

lobster &
crab

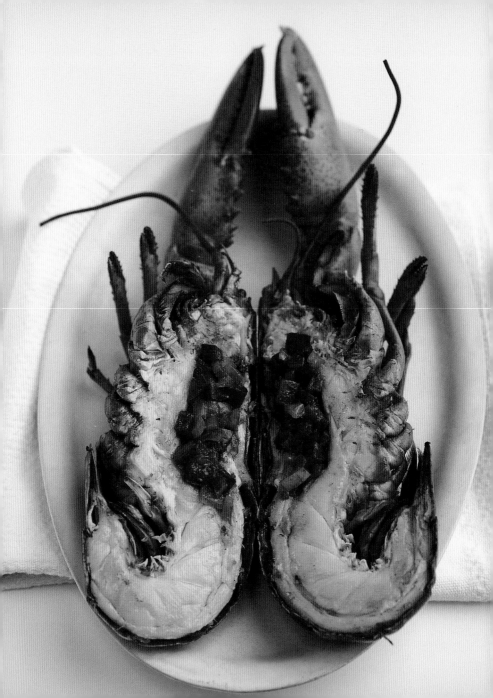

Grilled Lobster with Chilli Salsa

serves 4

2 cooked lobsters, about 650g (1lb 6oz) each

4 teaspoons olive oil

½ teaspoon Cayenne pepper

CHILLI SALSA

2 tablespoons olive oil

1 red capsicum (bell pepper), deseeded and diced

1 small onion, chopped

1 large red chilli, deseeded and finely chopped

1 tablespoon sun-dried tomato purée

salt and freshly ground black pepper

To make salsa, heat oil in a saucepan and fry red capsicum, onion and chilli for 5 minutes or until tender. Stir in the tomato purée and season to taste. Transfer to a bowl.

To cut lobsters in half lengthwise, turn one on its back. Cut through the head end first, using a large, sharp knife, then turn lobster round and cut through the tail end. Discard the small greyish sac in the head—everything else in the shell is edible. Crack the large claws with a small hammer or wooden rolling pin. Repeat with the second lobster. Drizzle the cut side of lobsters with oil and sprinkle with Cayenne pepper.

Heat a large non-stick frying pan or ridged cast-iron grill pan until very hot, then add lobster halves, cut-side down, and cook for 2–3 minutes, until lightly golden. Serve with salsa.

Sake-Simmered Lobster

serves 4

2 lobsters, about 450g (15oz) each

2 leeks, sliced into 15mm (½in) pieces

125g (4oz) watercress

8cm (3⅛in) piece fresh ginger

1 tablespoon fresh ginger juice

SIMMERING SAUCE

1¾ cups sake

7 tablespoons mirin

2 tablespoons dark soy sauce

2 tablespoons light soy sauce

2 tablespoons sugar

½ teaspoon salt

Cut lobsters in half lengthwise and then cut each half into 2–3 pieces.

Boil the leeks in salted water until just tender, and drain.

Blanch watercress in lightly salted boiling water, drain, and refresh in cold water. Drain again and cut into 4cm (1½in) lengths.

Slice ginger with the grain into very fine slivers and soak in cold water for 2–3 minutes.

To make simmering sauce, place sake and ¾ cup water in a saucepan and bring to a boil over high heat, then add all the remaining ingredients. Add lobster, and cover with a plate that fits down inside the pan and sits directly onto the food— this ensures even heat and flavour distribution by forcing the rising heat down. Boil for 5–6 minutes over high heat until the meat can be easily removed from the shell. Ladle simmering liquid over lobster several times. Add leek and watercress. Heat through, add the ginger juice, and remove immediately from heat. Serve garnished with slivers of ginger.

Lobster with Dill

serves 4

2 lobsters, about 750g (1lb 10oz) each

4 sprigs dill

1 lettuce

2 slices pineapple, fresh or canned

150g (5oz) button mushrooms

1 tablespoon mayonnaise

¾ cup thickened cream, lightly beaten

pinch of sugar

salt and white pepper

Prepare the lobsters for cooking (see Introduction) and add to a very large pan of boiling, slightly salted water. Cook for 15–20 minutes. Drain, take all the meat out of the shells and claws, and dice. Wash and dry the dill and snip off the small feathery leaves, reserving a little for decoration.

Wash and dry the lettuce. Drain the pineapple well and cut into small pieces. Slice the mushrooms wafer thin.

Place the lobster, pineapple, dill and mushrooms in a bowl and mix with the mayonnaise. Fold in the lightly beaten cream, flavoured with a pinch of sugar, salt and white pepper.

Line a large salad bowl with the lettuce leaves, spoon in the lobster mixture and decorate with the reserved dill.

Thai Steamed Crab

serves 4

4 blue swimmer crabs

2 large cloves garlic, crushed

2cm (¾in) piece fresh ginger, chopped

¼ cup coriander (cilantro) leaves, freshly chopped

1 teaspoon fish sauce

2 teaspoons soy sauce

200g (7oz) minced (ground) pork

sea salt and freshly ground black pepper

2 red chillies, sliced

1 spring onion, sliced

Carefully lift off the top shell of each crab, wash away the brains and yellow meats, and remove the white meat from the body, leaving legs intact. Set white meat aside. Rinse crab under running water to clean away any pieces of leftover shell. You should be left with a good, clean shell.

Combine crab meat, garlic, ginger, coriander, fish sauce, soy sauce and minced pork in a bowl. Mix together and season with salt and pepper. Evenly distribute the mixture between the 4 crab shells. Place the crabs into a steamer and cook for 10–15 minutes. The crab shell will turn from blue to a red colour.

Serve with the chillies, spring onions and extra coriander.

Lobster Provençale

serves 4

60g (2oz) butter

1 large clove garlic, crushed

2 spring onions, chopped

300g (10½oz) canned tomatoes

salt and freshly ground black
pepper

pinch of saffron threads

1 large lobster, cooked

3 tablespoons brandy

3 cups boiled rice

½ bunch chives, chopped

In a shallow frying pan, melt butter over a moderate heat. Add garlic, spring onions, tomatoes, salt, pepper and saffron. Cook until onions are translucent, about 2 minutes.

Remove meat from lobster and cut into large pieces. Add lobster to frying pan and flame with the brandy. Cook gently until lobster is heated through.

Place rice on serving plate and sprinkle with chives.

Remove lobster from frying pan, retaining the cooking liquid as a sauce.

Arrange the lobster on the rice and spoon the cooking liquid over lobster. Serve with lemon wedges.

Singapore Chilli Crab

serves 4

2 raw mud crabs, weighing about
  1kg (2lb 3oz) each

2 tablespoons sambal oelek (chilli
  paste)

⅓ cup tomato sauce

⅓ cup chilli sauce

2 tablespoons oyster sauce

1 tablespoon sugar

1 teaspoon salt

1 tablespoon vegetable oil

6 cloves garlic, minced

2 cups hot chicken stock

2 egg whites

¼ cup coriander (cilantro) leaves

Prepare the crab (see Introduction). Cut the body section into 4 pieces and crack the large claw shells with the back of a heavy knife. Wash the crab and drain. Scrub the back shell and keep it whole to use as a garnish.

Combine the sambal oelek, tomato sauce and chilli sauce in a small bowl. Combine the oyster sauce, sugar and salt in another.

Heat a wok over medium-high heat and add the oil. Fry the garlic for 10 seconds, stirring constantly.

Add the chilli mixture and cook for another 10 seconds, stirring. Add the stock and oyster sauce mixture and stir again.

Increase heat to high and bring to a fast boil. Add the crab pieces (including the back shell), stir to settle it into the liquid and cook for 3 minutes, stirring occasionally and turning the larger pieces once. Remove the back shell.

Drizzle in the egg white and stir gently until there are white streaks through the sauce.

Place on a serving dish, arrange the back shell on top and garnish with coriander leaves. Serve with Chinese steamed or baked buns, rice or bread and a finger bowl.

Lobster à L'Américane

serves 4

1 lobster, about 1kg (2lb 3oz)

2 tablespoons olive oil

90g (3oz) butter, softened

½ cup brandy

6 French shallots

1 cup dry white wine

1 cup fish stock, heated

4 tomatoes, blanched, peeled, deseeded and chopped

1 sprig tarragon

¼ cup parsley, finely chopped

salt and freshly ground black pepper

Buy a live lobster if possible and prepare it (see Introduction). Chop into fairly large pieces, shell and all, collecting and reserving the juices. Discard the sac and remove the intestinal tract, but reserve the coral, if any.

Fry the lobster pieces briskly in olive oil, stirring in 30g (1oz) of the butter until their shell has turned bright orange-red. Drain off excess butter and pour in the brandy. Heat and flame.

Peel and finely chop the shallots and sweat in 30g (1oz) of the butter in a wide, fairly deep pan. Add the white wine and continue cooking until the wine has evaporated.

Add the lobster pieces, their reserved juice and the hot fish stock. Add the tomatoes and the sprig of tarragon. Simmer for 15 minutes. Work the coral into the remaining butter. Remove the lobster pieces with a slotted spoon and place in a heated serving dish. Discard the tarragon.

Add the coral butter to the sauce in the pan, stir gently as the butter melts, and add the chopped parsley. Season to taste with salt and freshly ground pepper, pour over the lobster and serve at once.

Lobster Mornay

serves 4

2 medium lobsters, cooked and
halved

MORNAY SAUCE
1¼ cups milk

1 bay leaf

1 small onion, chopped

5 black peppercorns

30g (1oz) butter, plus 15g (½oz)

2 tablespoons plain flour

¼ cup cream

65g (2⅓oz) Cheddar cheese,
grated

salt and freshly ground black
pepper

65g (2⅓oz) fresh breadcrumbs

Remove the lobster meat from the shells and cut
into bite-size pieces. Reserve the shells.

In a saucepan, place the milk, bay leaf, onion
and peppercorns. Heat slowly to boiling point.
Remove from the heat, cover and stand for 10
minutes. Strain.

In a pan, melt 30g (1oz) butter, then remove from
the heat. Stir in the flour and blend, gradually
adding the strained milk. Return the pan to the
heat, and stir constantly until the sauce boils and
thickens. Simmer for 1 minute, remove from the
heat, add the cream, cheese, salt and pepper.
Stir the sauce until the cheese melts, then add
the lobster.

Divide the mixture between the shells. Melt
the remaining butter in a small pan, add the
breadcrumbs, and stir to combine. Scatter the
crumbs over the lobster and brown under a hot
grill.

Scampi with Basil Butter

serves 4

8 raw scampi or yabbies, heads
  removed

BASIL BUTTER
90g (3oz) butter, melted

¼ cup fresh basil, chopped

1 clove garlic, crushed

2 teaspoons honey

Cut scampi or yabbies in half lengthwise.

To make basil butter, place butter, basil, garlic and honey in a small bowl and whisk to combine.

Brush each cut side of scampi or yabbie with basil butter and cook under a preheated hot grill for 2 minutes or until they change colour and are tender. Drizzle with any remaining basil butter and serve immediately.

mussels & clams

Belgian-Style Mussels

serves 4

2kg (4lb 6oz) mussels in their shells

30g (1oz) butter

1 tablespoon vegetable oil

4 French shallots, chopped

2 stalks celery, chopped, plus any leaves

⅔ cup dry white wine

freshly ground black pepper

½ cup thickened cream

½ cup fresh flat-leaf parsley, chopped

Scrub the mussels under cold running water, then pull away any beards and discard any mussels that are open or damaged. Heat the butter and oil in a very large saucepan, then add the shallots or onion and celery and cook for 2–3 minutes until the shallots are translucent.

Stir in the wine and plenty of pepper and bring to the boil. Add the mussels, cover and cook over a high heat, shaking the pan occasionally, for 4–5 minutes until the mussels have opened. Remove from the pan and keep warm in a bowl, discarding any that remain closed.

Roughly chop the celery leaves, reserving a few for garnish. Add the chopped leaves, cream and parsley to the cooking juices and season again if necessary. Bring to the boil, then spoon over the mussels. Garnish with celery leaves.

Clam and Black Mussel Broth

serves 4

2 tablespoons vegetable oil

1 onion, finely chopped

2 tablespoons tom yum paste

500g (17½oz) surf clams, cleaned
and free of sand

500g (17½oz) black mussels,
cleaned

2 cups chicken stock

1 stalk lemongrass, bruised

juice of 1 lime

¼ cup coriander (cilantro) stalks
and roots, finely chopped

1 tablespoon fish sauce

¼ cup fresh coriander (cilantro)
leaves, roughly chopped

Heat the oil in a wok or large cooking pot. Add
the onion, tom yum, clams and mussels. Simmer,
covered, for 30 seconds.

Add the chicken stock, lemongrass, lime juice,
coriander stalks and roots, fish sauce and stir
through. Cook until all the shells have opened.

Add the fresh coriander leaves, remove the
lemongrass and serve in soup bowls.

Clams Waterzooi

serves 4

1 tablespoon olive oil

1kg (2lb 3oz) clams, cleaned

1½ cups dry white wine

5 cups chicken or fish stock

250g (9oz) desiree potatoes,
    peeled and cut large dice

150g (5oz) carrots, peeled and
    finely sliced

150g (5oz) leeks (white part only),
    sliced and washed

150g (5oz) celery, washed and
    sliced

1 tablespoon cornflour
    (cornstarch)

⅓ cup thickened cream

salt and freshly ground black
    pepper

¼ cup parsley, chopped

Place the oil, clams and white wine in a large pot over high heat. Cook until all have opened.

Remove the clams and set aside.

Add the stock to the broth in the pot, bring to the boil, add the potatoes and cook for 10 minutes.

Add the carrots, leeks, and celery and cook until the potatoes are cooked, around 8–10 minutes.

Strain the cooking liquid out of the vegetables and pour it into another pot on high heat. Keep the vegetables and potatoes aside.

Bring the pot to the boil. Combine the cornflour with 2 tablespoons water, add to the pot and boil until thickened, around 1 minute. Add the cream, salt and pepper and boil for another 30 seconds.

Add the clams and vegetables, bring back to the boil, then serve in a large soup bowl or in individual plates. Garnish with parsley. Serve with dry white wine.

Leek and Seeded Mustard Mussels

serves 4

30g (1oz) butter

1 large leek (white part only), finely sliced

1kg (2lb 3oz) black mussels, cleaned

3 tablespoons seeded mustard

½ cup dry white wine

2 tablespoons thickened cream

¼ cup parsley, chopped

salt and freshly ground black pepper

Place butter in a pot over high heat. Add leek and cook for 1 minute.

Add mussels, seeded mustard and white wine.

Cook mussels until all have opened, stirring frequently.

Add cream and parsley, stir for 15 seconds on high heat. Season with salt and pepper to taste.

Saffron and Surf Clam Risotto

serves 4

½ cup virgin olive oil

1 onion, finely sliced

4 cloves garlic, finely chopped

400g (14oz) Arborio rice

1½ cups dry white wine

pinch of saffron threads

2 cups chicken stock

salt and freshly ground black
    pepper

¼ cup mixed fresh herbs, chopped

500g (17½oz) pipis

500g (17½oz) surf clams

On medium heat, put the virgin olive oil, onion
and garlic in a large pot and cook for 1 minute,
covered.

Add the rice and stir with a wooden spatula.

Add the white wine and saffron and cook slowly
until the rice starts becoming dry, around 5
minutes.

Add the chicken stock, seasoning, mixed herbs,
pipis and surf clams and cook until all the shells
have opened and the rice is cooked, around 15
minutes. Keep stirring frequently to avoid the rice
sticking to the pot.

Serve with salad and crispy ciabatta bread.

Mussels with Tomatoes and Wine

serves 4

1kg (2lb 3oz) fresh mussels,
  scrubbed and beards removed

1 French shallot, chopped

1 cup dry white wine

½ small bunch fresh chives,
  chopped

TOMATO AND SMOKED
SALMON SAUCE

2 teaspoons olive oil

2 cloves garlic, crushed

2 French shallots, chopped

3 slices smoked salmon, sliced
  into thin strips

1 red capsicum (bell pepper),
  sliced

1 tablespoon tomato paste

400g (14oz) canned diced
  tomatoes

¼ cup fresh parsley, chopped

For the sauce, heat the oil in a non-stick frying pan over a medium heat. Add the garlic and shallots. Cook, stirring, for 1–2 minutes. Add the salmon and red capsicum. Cook, stirring, for 3 minutes. Stir in the tomato paste. Cook for 3–4 minutes or until it becomes deep red and develops a rich aroma. Add the tomatoes. Cook, stirring, for 5 minutes or until the mixture starts to thicken. Stir in the parsley. Keep warm.

Meanwhile, place the mussels, shallot and wine in a large saucepan over a high heat. Cover. Bring to the boil then reduce the heat. Cook for 5 minutes or until the mussels open. Discard any mussels that do not open.

Add the sauce to the mussels. Toss to combine.

To serve, divide the mixture between deep bowls and scatter with chives. Accompany with crusty bread and a glass of red wine.

Spaghetti Vongole

serves 4

300g (10½oz) spaghetti

3 tablespoons virgin olive oil

1 onion, very finely chopped

2 cloves garlic, finely chopped

500g (17½oz) clams, cleaned and
sand removed

½cup white wine

salt and freshly ground black
pepper

¼ cup fresh oregano, chopped

Bring a large saucepan of salted water to the
boil, add the pasta and cook for 8 minutes or until
just firm in the centre (al dente). Refresh in cold
water, stir with half the oil and set aside.

Heat the remaining oil in a large cooking pot over
high heat. Add the onion and garlic and cook for
1 minute.

Add the clams, white wine, salt and pepper.

When all the clams have opened, add the
spaghetti and oregano. Cook for another 2
minutes, then serve.

Laksa

serves 4

2 tablespooons peanut or
    vegetable oil

1 onion, finely chopped

3 cloves garlic, chopped

1 tablespoon laksa paste

1¾ cups chicken stock

1 stalk lemongrass, bruised

1kg (2lb 3oz) mussels, cleaned

1 cup coconut cream

150g (5oz) rice noodles

1 kaffir lime leaf, finely chopped

Place oil, onion, garlic and laksa paste in a large saucepan on medium heat and cook for 3–5 minutes.

Add chicken stock, lemongrass and mussels and cook until mussels start to open.

Add coconut cream, rice noodles and lime leaf. Cook for another 4 minutes until all mussels have opened. Discard the lemongrass and any mussels that do not open.

Dijon Mussels

serves 4

30g (1oz) butter

½ onion, finely chopped

½ bunch celery, finely chopped

½ leek, finely chopped

1kg (2lb 3oz) mussels, cleaned

1 cup dry white wine

1 cup thickened cream

1 tablespoon Dijon mustard

freshly ground black pepper

¼ cup parsley, chopped

Melt butter over a high heat in a saucepan, add onion, celery and leek and cook for 1 minute. Add mussels and white wine and cover.

Mix cream and mustard together and add to the saucepan. Season with pepper.

Stir frequently to ensure even cooking of mussels. When mussels have opened, add parsley. Discard any mussels that do not open, and serve.

Clams Provençale

serves 4

¼ cup extra virgin olive oil

1 onion, finely chopped

1 red capsicum (bell pepper), diced

4 tomatoes, diced

½ stalk celery, sliced

2 cloves garlic, chopped

1kg (2lb 3oz) surf clams, cleaned and sand removed

¾ cup dry white wine

8 sprigs rosemary, leaves removed and chopped

salt and freshly ground black pepper

Place oil, onion, red capsicum, tomatoes, celery and garlic in a large saucepan and cook over a high heat for 5 minutes, stirring occasionally to avoid sticking.

Add surf clams, white wine, rosemary and seasoning, cover and cook until all shells have opened. Stir frequently to ensure even cooking.

When clams are open, serve in large bowls with a salad or grilled baguette.

Mussels Marinières

serves 4

1kg (2lb 3oz) mussels, cleaned

1 small onion, sliced

1 stalk celery, sliced

1 clove garlic, chopped

¼ cup white wine

freshly ground black pepper

15g (½oz) butter

¼ cup parsley, chopped

Put mussels in a casserole with onion, celery, garlic and wine.

Cook until mussels have opened, stirring frequently to make sure mussels are cooked evenly.

Season with pepper, then add butter and parsley to mussels and stir. Serve immediately with fresh crusty bread.

oysters & scallops

Oysters Acapulco

serves 4

CORIANDER (CILANTRO) PESTO

½ cup coriander (cilantro) leaves

2 tablespoons pine nuts, toasted

1 clove garlic, roughly chopped

20g (⅔oz) Parmesan cheese, grated

20g (⅔oz) pecorino cheese, grated

¼ cup olive oil

salt and freshly ground black pepper

OYSTERS

24 oysters in the half shell

rock salt (optional)

¼ cup coriander (cilantro) pesto

red capsicum (bell pepper), finely diced

40g (1½oz) cacique or fetta cheese, crumbled

To make the coriander pesto, place the coriander, pine nuts, garlic and cheeses in a food processor and process until a paste. With the motor still running, add oil in a steady stream until well combined.

Season with salt and pepper to taste. Store in refrigerator with a little olive oil over top to prevent coriander going brown.

Heat grill. If grilling oysters, make a bed of rock salt in 2 baking pans and arrange the oysters in them. If barbecueing, the oysters will go directly on the grill.

Top each oyster with coriander pesto, red capsicum and crumbled cheese. Cook under grill until cheese has lightly browned.

Poached Scallops with Ginger

serves 4

500g (17½oz) fresh scallops

4 green onions

1 medium carrot

4 sprigs flat-leaf parsley

¼ cup lemon juice

1 teaspoon soy sauce

2 teaspoons honey

2cm (¾in) piece fresh ginger, grated

Remove any dark membrane from the scallops, leaving coral attached. Rinse well.

Wash and peel green onions and carrot, then cut into julienne strips. Pluck the parsley leaves from the stalks and rinse.

Heat ¾ cup water, the lemon juice, soy sauce, honey and ginger to simmering point. Add the scallops, carrots, green onions and parsley and poach for 3–4 minutes. Do not overcook.

Remove to individual scallop shells or entrée dishes with a slotted spoon. Strain the poaching liquid, return to the saucepan and reduce over quick heat to intensify the flavour. Spoon over the scallops and serve immediately.

Oysters Kilpatrick

serves 4

24 oysters in the half shell

1 teaspoon Worcestershire sauce

1 cup cream

salt and freshly ground black
  pepper

250g (9oz) bacon strips, finely
  chopped

fine breadcrumbs

Remove oysters from shells and put aside. Put shells on a baking sheet and heat in a moderate oven. Mix Worcestershire sauce and cream. When shells are hot, return oysters to shells. Use tongs to handle the shells, as they get very hot. Add a little of the cream mixture to each shell and sprinkle with salt and pepper.

Top each oyster with chopped bacon and fine breadcrumbs. Place under a hot grill and grill until bacon is crisp but not burnt and oysters are warmed through.

Note Oysters Kilpatrick are very tasty served with a bowl of hot puréed spinach and thin slices of buttered brown or rye bread.

Scallops in Filo with Lemon Butter

serves 4

SAUCE

15g (½oz) butter

4 French shallots, minced

½ cup dry white wine

2 tablespoons thickened cream

SCALLOPS

6 sheets filo pastry

90g (3oz) butter, melted, plus 30g (1oz)

8 large scallops

1 tablespoon brandy

salt and freshly ground black pepper

1 egg yolk

2 tablespoons lemon juice

To make the sauce, melt butter in a small heavy saucepan over medium heat. Add shallots and sauté for 3 minutes.

Add wine and boil for 5 minutes or until liquid is reduced to ¼ cup.

Stir in cream.

Preheat oven to 220°C (420°F). Place 1 filo sheet on work surface (keep remaining filo covered). Brush with melted butter.

Top with second sheet. Brush with melted butter.

Top with third sheet. Cut filo stack into four 15cm (6in) squares.

Place one scallop in center of each square. Brush scallops with brandy. Season.

Pull up all sides of filo around scallops to form pouches. Pinch center to seal. Repeat with remaining filo and scallops.

Arrange pouches on baking sheet. Brush with melted butter. Bake pouches for 10 minutes or until golden.

Reheat sauce over medium-low heat. Whisk in yolk—do not boil. Add 30g (1oz) butter and whisk until just melted. Add lemon juice and season with salt and pepper. Spoon sauce onto plates and top with pastry pouches.

Oysters Rockefeller

serves 4

rock salt

24 medium oysters in shell

½ medium onion, finely chopped

½ cup parsley, chopped

1 stalk celery, finely chopped

90g (3oz) butter

40g (1½oz) fresh spinach,
   chopped

⅔ cup dry breadcrumbs

½ teaspoon salt

10 drops red pepper sauce

pinch of ground anise

Preheat oven to 230°C (450°F). Fill two 23cm (9in) glass pie dishes with rock salt to 1cm (¼in) deep, then sprinkle with water. Scrub oysters in shell under running cold water, then open and remove from shell (see the Introduction).

Remove any bits of shell and place oyster on deep half of shell. Arrange filled shells on rock salt bases. In a saucepan, cook onion, parsley and celery in butter, stirring constantly, until onion is tender.

Mix in remaining ingredients. Spoon about 1 tablespoon spinach mixture onto each oyster. Bake for 10 minutes and serve immediately.

Steamed Scallops with Black Bean

serves 4

12 large or 24 small scallops in
  half shells

1 tablespoon dry sherry

1 tablespoon Chinese salted black
  beans

1 large garlic, crushed

3 teaspoons soy sauce

¼ teaspoon salt

pinch of freshly ground black
  pepper

½ teaspoon sugar

1 teaspoon olive oil

1 teaspoon cornflour (cornstarch)

1 tablespoon sesame oil

1 green onion (green part only),
  cut into fine slices

12 coriander (cilantro) leaves

½ hot chilli, deseeded and cut into
  5mm (⅛in) diamond shapes

Use the scallop shells for the cooking and serving dishes. Mix scallops with the sherry, then place 1 scallop in each shell. Set aside.

Soak the black beans in cold water for 15 minutes, then rinse, dry on absorbent paper, and mince. Combine beans, garlic, soy sauce, salt, pepper, sugar, oil and cornflour. Distribute some of this mixture over each of the scallops, and trickle the sesame oil on top.

Bring a few inches of water to a vigorous boil in a steamer. Place the scallops on a steamer rack, cover tightly, and steam for 5 minutes. Remove, sprinkle with green onions, and garnish each scallop with coriander (cilantro) and a hot chilli diamond before serving.

Tempura Oysters

serves 4

24 oysters

sunflower oil for deep frying

DIPPING SAUCE

⅓ cup dark soy sauce

juice of 1 lime

TEMPURA BATTER

½ cup cornstarch (cornflour)

½ cup plain (all-purpose) flour

small pinch of salt

4 teaspoons toasted sesame seeds

¾ cup ice cold soda water

1 lime, cut into wedges

Open all the oysters (see Introduction) and pour off any liquid. Carefully cut the meat out of the deeper shells and retain the shells for serving.

To make the dipping sauce, combine the soy sauce and lime juice with ¹/₃ cup water and pour into 4 dipping saucers.

Heat the sunflower oil to 190°C (375°F).

Make the batter by sifting the cornstarch, flour and salt into a mixing bowl. Stir in the sesame seeds then stir in the ice cold soda water until just mixed. Add a little more water if it seems too thick. The batter should be very thin and almost transparent.

Dip the oysters one at a time into the batter. Drop into the hot oil and fry for a minute until crisp and golden. Lift out and drain on absorbent paper.

Return the oysters to their shells and arrange on plates. Serve with lime wedges and the dipping sauce.

Seared Scallop Salad

serves 4

2 teaspoons sesame oil

2 cloves garlic, crushed

400g (14oz) scallops, cleaned

4 rashers bacon, chopped

1 cos lettuce, leaves separated

50g (1¾oz) croutons

40g (1½oz) Parmesan cheese,
   shaved

MUSTARD DRESSING

3 tablespoons mayonnaise

1 tablespoon olive oil

1 tablespoon vinegar

2 teaspoons Dijon
   mustard

To make dressing, place mayonnaise, olive oil, vinegar and mustard in a bowl, mix to combine and set aside.

Heat sesame oil in a frying pan over a high heat, add garlic and scallops and cook, stirring, for 1 minute or until scallops just turn opaque. Remove scallop mixture from pan and set aside. Add bacon to pan and cook, stirring, for 4 minutes or until crisp. Remove bacon from pan and drain on absorbent paper.

Place lettuce leaves in a large salad bowl, add dressing and toss to coat. Add bacon, croutons and Parmesan and toss to combine. Spoon scallop mixture over salad and serve.

Grilled Oysters with Champagne

serves 4

12 fresh oysters in their shells,
   pre-shucked

½ cup fish stock

¼ cup Champagne

30g (1oz) butter

2 tablespoons thickened cream

freshly ground black pepper

50g (1¾oz) baby spinach

Place the oyster shells in a flameproof dish lined with crumpled foil so that the shells sit level.

Bring the fish stock to a simmer and poach the oysters for 30–60 seconds, until just firm. Remove oysters from the pan, add the Champagne and boil for 2 minutes to reduce. Remove from the heat and whisk in the butter, then the cream. Season with pepper.

Preheat the grill to high. Cook the spinach in a saucepan of water for 2–3 minutes until wilted. Squeeze out the excess liquid and divide between the shells. Top with an oyster and spoon over a little sauce. Cook close to the grill for 1 minute or until heated through.

squid & octopus

Calamari in Garlic and Capers

serves 4

1 carrot, peeled and chopped

1 onion, chopped

½ bunch thyme

8 cloves garlic

juice and zest of 1 lemon

100g (3½oz) capers

4 calamari tubes

MARINADE

1 teaspoon cumin

¾ cup extra virgin olive oil

juice of 2 lemons

1 teaspoon salt

½ teaspoon ground black pepper

8 sprigs lemon thyme

SALAD

2 heads radicchio

1 endive

2 teaspoons capers

½ cup flat-leaf parsley, chopped

Place carrot, onion, thyme, garlic, lemon juice and zest, capers and 4 cups water in a saucepan, bring to the boil and simmer for 10 minutes.

Clean the calamari tubes under running water. Place into the simmering poaching liquid for approximately 2 minutes.

Remove the garlic cloves from the poaching liquid and slice. Place the ingredients for the marinade in a bowl, add the sliced garlic and mix together.

Remove calamari from the poaching liquid and cut into 5cm-wide (2in) strips. Place into the marinade and leave in the refrigerator for 30 minutes.

Wash the radicchio and endive, discard the outer leaves, place in a bowl and mix with the capers and parsley.

Remove the calamari from the marinade and add to the salad. Use ¼ cup of the marinade as a dressing. Serve immediately.

Calamari with Lemon and Herb

serves 4

⅓ cup lemon juice

3 cloves garlic, crushed

½ cup olive oil

1kg (2lb 3oz) calamari, cut into
  thin rings

DRESSING

⅓ cup lemon juice

⅓ cup olive oil

¼ cup parsley, chopped

1 clove garlic, crushed

1 teaspoon Dijon mustard

salt and freshly ground black
  pepper

Place lemon juice, garlic and oil in a bowl, add
the calamari and marinate for at least 3 hours. If
time permits, marinate overnight.

To make the dressing, place all ingredients in a
bowl or jar and whisk well until dressing thickens
slightly.

Heat a little oil in a pan, add the calamari, and
cook for a few minutes until cooked through.
Alternatively, the calamari can be cooked on a
chargrill plate.

Serve calamari with lemon and herb dressing
drizzled over.

Paella

serves 6

½ teaspoon saffron threads

1 tablespoon olive oil

375g (13oz) chicken breast fillets, diced

1 onion, finely chopped

3 cloves garlic, freshly crushed

1 small red capsicum (bell pepper), diced

1 small green capsicum (bell pepper), diced

2 cups bomba rice

4 cups chicken stock

12 raw prawns (shrimp), shelled and deveined, tails left intact

250g (9oz) calamari rings

250g (9oz) mussels, scrubbed and beards removed

¾ cup frozen peas, thawed

¼ cup fresh parsley, chopped

1 lemon, cut into wedges

Combine the saffron threads and 2 tablespoons boiling water in a small bowl. Leave to stand for 5 minutes.

Meanwhile, heat the oil in a large saucepan over medium-high heat. Cook the chicken for 2–3 minutes or until golden. Add the onion, garlic, and red and green capsicums and cook for 2–3 minutes.

Add the rice, saffron mixture and 3 cups of chicken stock. Bring to a boil, cover and simmer over low heat for 15 minutes, stirring from time to time.

Add the prawns (shrimp), calamari, mussels, peas, parsley and remaining stock. Cook for a further 8–10 minutes, stirring from time to time, or until the rice is tender and the seafood is cooked. Serve immediately with lemon wedges.

Spicy Deep-Fried Squid Rings

serves 4

6 tablespoons plain (all-purpose) flour

2 tablespoons paprika

1 teaspoon salt

500g (17½oz) fresh squid, cut into rings, or frozen squid rings, defrosted and dried

vegetable oil for deep-frying

Mix together the flour, paprika and salt. Toss the squid rings in the seasoned flour to coat evenly.

Heat 5cm (2in) of vegetable oil in a large heavy-based saucepan. Test that the oil is ready by adding a squid ring—it should sizzle at once. Cook a quarter of the rings for 1–2 minutes, until golden. Drain on absorbent paper and keep warm while you cook the remaining rings in 3 more batches. Serve with mayonnaise.

Sambal Goreng Sotong

serves 4

2 teaspoons tamarind pulp

5 large red dried chillies, deseeded

¼ teaspoon shrimp paste

5 candlenuts

4 French shallots, coarsely
   chopped

5 medium squid

1 tablespoon peanut oil

1–2 stalks lemongrass, bruised

2 teaspoon palm sugar, grated

salt

Soak the tamarind pulp in ¼ cup hot water. Strain when cool and discard the pulp.

To make the spice paste, toast the chillies in a dry pan until crisp. Toast the shrimp paste over a gas flame or wrap in foil and lightly toast over an electric element.

Grind the chillies and candlenuts to a powder in a mortar and pestle or small food processor. Add the shallots and shrimp paste and continue to grind to a paste.

Cut each squid tube in half and score on the inside, horizontally and vertically. Slice diagonally into strips about 3cm (1⅛in) wide. Cut the tentacles into 2–3cm (1– 1⅛in) lengths and the head section into quarters.

Heat a wok over medium-low heat and add the oil. Add the spice paste and lemongrass and fry, stirring constantly for 3–5 minutes until the oil starts to separate. Stir in the tamarind liquid and palm sugar.

Add the prepared squid and stir. Reduce heat to low and cook uncovered, stirring frequently for about 6 minutes until the squid is cooked. Remove the lemongrass, add salt to taste and serve.

Char-Grilled Baby Octopus Salad

serves 4

375g (13oz) baby octopus, cleaned

1 teaspoon sesame oil

1 tablespoon lime juice

¼ cup sweet chilli sauce

1 tablespoon fish sauce

60g (2oz) rice noodle vermicelli

125g (4oz) mixed salad leaves

1 cup bean sprouts

1 Lebanese cucumber, halved

200g (7oz) cherry tomatoes, halved

½ cup fresh coriander (cilantro) sprigs

2 limes, cut into wedges

Rinse the cleaned octopus and pat dry with absorbent paper.

Put the sesame oil, lime juice, sweet chilli sauce and fish sauce in a jug and whisk to combine. Pour over the octopus and coat with the marinade. Cover with cling wrap and marinate for 4 hours or overnight. Drain and reserve the marinade.

Put the vermicelli in a bowl, cover with boiling water and allow to stand for 10 minutes or until soft. Drain well.

Divide the mixed salad leaves among 4 plates, top with the bean sprouts, rice vermicelli, cucumber and tomatoes.

Cook the octopus on a preheated chargrill or barbecue until tender and well coloured. Put the marinade in a small pot and bring to the boil. Serve the octopus on top of the salad, drizzle with the hot marinade and garnish with coriander and lime wedges.

Seafood Curry

serves 4

1 tablespoon peanut oil

½ teaspoon ground turmeric

1 teaspoon ground coriander

1 cup coconut milk

2 tablespoons lime juice

2 teaspoons palm sugar or brown sugar

2 lime leaves, shredded

400g (14oz) ling fillets, diced

200g (7oz) raw prawns (shrimp), heads removed and shelled

200g (7oz) squid rings

PASTE

2 French shallots, chopped

2 cloves garlic, chopped

2cm (¾in) piece fresh ginger, chopped

3 medium chillies, deseeded and sliced

1 stalk lemongrass, very thinly sliced

½ teaspoon salt

Grind or pound paste ingredients in a mortar and pestle or food processor.

Heat oil in a wok or large frying pan. Add paste and cook for 1–2 minutes. Add turmeric and coriander and cook until aromatic. Add coconut milk, ¼ cup water, the lime juice, palm sugar and lime leaves. Bring to the boil, add seafood and cook for 3–4 minutes or until tender. Serve with noodles or rice.

Octopus with Potatoes and Peas

serves 4

1kg (2lb 3oz) octopus

salt

½ cup olive oil

1 large onion, chopped

4 cloves garlic, chopped

400g (14oz) canned tomatoes

¼ teaspoon ground chilli

500g (17½oz) potatoes, peeled
  and cut into thick slices

250g (9oz) frozen peas, thawed

Put octopus in a large saucepan without adding water. Sprinkle with salt, cover, and let cook in its own juices over a low heat for about 45 minutes. After 10 minutes, lift the octopus out with a fork and dip into a pan of boiling water, then run the octopus under cold water and return it to the saucepan to continue cooking. Repeat process every 10 minutes, 4 times in total.

Heat olive oil in a casserole dish, add onion and gently fry for 1 minute. Add garlic, tomatoes with juice and chilli powder, cook for about 10 minutes. Add the potatoes and cook for about 5 minutes. Add the octopus and its cooking liquid.

Add salt to taste and cook gently, uncovered, for about 20 minutes, then add the peas and cook 10 minutes more until potatoes and peas are tender and sauce is reduced. Serve the octopus and vegetables straight from the casserole.

Thai Squid Salad

serves 4

3 squid tubes, cleaned

200g (7oz) green beans, sliced lengthwise

2 tomatoes, cut into wedges

1 small green pawpaw, peeled, deseeded and shredded

4 spring onions, sliced

1 cup mint leaves

1 cup coriander (cilantro) leaves

1 fresh red chilli, chopped

LIME DRESSING

2 teaspoons brown sugar

3 tablespoons lime juice

1 tablespoon fish sauce

Using a sharp knife, make a single cut down the length of each squid tube and open out. Score parallel lines down the length of squid, taking care not to cut through the flesh. Score in the opposite direction to form a diamond pattern.

Heat a non-stick chargrill or frying pan over a high heat, add squid and cook for 1–2 minutes each side or until tender. Remove from pan and cut into thin strips.

Place squid, beans, tomatoes, pawpaw, spring onions, mint, coriander and chilli in a serving bowl.

To make dressing, place sugar, lime juice and fish sauce in a screw-top jar and shake well. Drizzle over salad and toss to combine. Cover and stand for 20 minutes before serving.

Barbecued Octopus and Potato Salad

serves 6

500g (17½oz) baby octopus,
    cleaned

500g (17½oz) pink-skinned
    potatoes

100g (3½oz) rocket or mixed salad
    greens

2 Lebanese cucumbers, chopped

2 green onions, finely sliced

LIME AND CHILLI MARINADE
2 tablespoons olive oil

juice of 1 lime

1 fresh red chilli, diced

1 clove garlic, crushed

TOMATO CONCASSE
4 Roma tomatoes, diced

½ cup fresh coriander (cilantro),
    chopped

½ red onion, diced

⅓ cup balsamic or sherry vinegar

1 tablespoon olive oil

1 tablespoon lemon juice

freshly ground black pepper

To make marinade, place oil, lime juice, chilli and garlic in a bowl. Mix to combine. Cut octopus in half lengthwise—if very small, leave whole. Add to marinade. Marinate in the refrigerator overnight or at least 2 hours. Cook potatoes until tender. Drain and cool slightly, then cut into bite-size chunks.

To make concasse, place tomatoes, coriander, onion, vinegar, oil, lemon juice and black pepper in a bowl. Mix to combine.

Line a serving platter with rocket leaves. Top with potatoes, cucumber and onions. Preheat a barbecue hotplate or chargrill pan to very hot. Drain octopus and cook on barbecue or in pan, turning frequently, for 3–5 minutes or until tentacles curl—take care not to overcook or octopus will be tough.

To serve, spoon hot octopus over prepared salad. Top with concasse and accompany with crusty bread.

Pan-Fried Squid with Lemon

serves 4

680g (1lb 6oz) squid tubes

½ cup fine semolina

1 teaspoon salt

1 teaspoon freshly ground black
  pepper

1 cup olive oil

1 lemon, cut into wedges

Cut each squid tube along 1 side. With a sharp knife, score inside skin diagonally in both directions, making a diamond pattern. Cut squid into 2 x 4cm (¾ x 1½in) rectangles.

In a bowl, combine semolina, salt and pepper.

Heat oil in a large frying pan or wok until hot. Dip squid into semolina and cook in batches until lightly brown and crisp. Drain on absorbent paper and serve with lemon wedges.

whole fish

Chinese-Style Steamed Grey Mullet

serves 4

2 grey mullet, about 680g (1lb 6oz) each

2 teaspoons salt

2 tablespoons vegetable oil

2 tablespoons light soy sauce

1 large carrot, cut into fine strips

8 spring onions, cut into fine strips

8cm (3⅛in) piece fresh ginger, grated

2 tablespoons sesame oil

¼ cup fresh coriander (cilantro) leaves

Scale and gut the mullet (see Introduction), then clean and pat dry. Make 4 deep slashes along each side of the fish, then rub the fish inside and out with salt, vegetable oil and soy sauce. Cover and place in the refrigerator for 30 minutes.

Spread half the carrot, spring onions and ginger on a large piece of foil. Place fish on top, then sprinkle with remaining vegetables and ginger and any remaining marinade. Loosely fold over foil to seal. Transfer fish to a steamer.

Cook for 20 minutes or until the fish is firm and cooked through. Heat sesame oil in a small saucepan, drizzle over fish and garnish with coriander.

Dover Sole with Lemon and Parsley

serves 4

4 Dover sole (or dory), about 375g (13oz) each

75g (2½oz) butter

2 teaspoons salt flakes

freshly ground black pepper

juice of 1 lemon

¼ cup fresh parsley, chopped

Preheat the oven to 200°C (400°F). Lightly oil a large baking sheet. Scale, gut and clean the fish (see Introduction).

Cut away the 'frill' of fins along each side of the fish with a pair of scissors. With a sharp knife, score a line about 1cm (½in) from the sides of the fish, on both sides.

Melt the butter in a small saucepan. Place the fish, dark-side up, on the baking sheet, brush with melted butter, then sprinkle with the salt flakes and pepper. Reserve the remaining melted butter. Bake the fish for 15 minutes or until the flesh is white and cooked through.

Add the lemon juice, parsley and any cooking juices to the reserved butter and heat through, stirring. Spoon over the sole.

Note Dover sole should be treated simply — butter, parsley, lemon juice and seasoning are all it needs. Scoring the fish before cooking makes it easier to remove the skin.

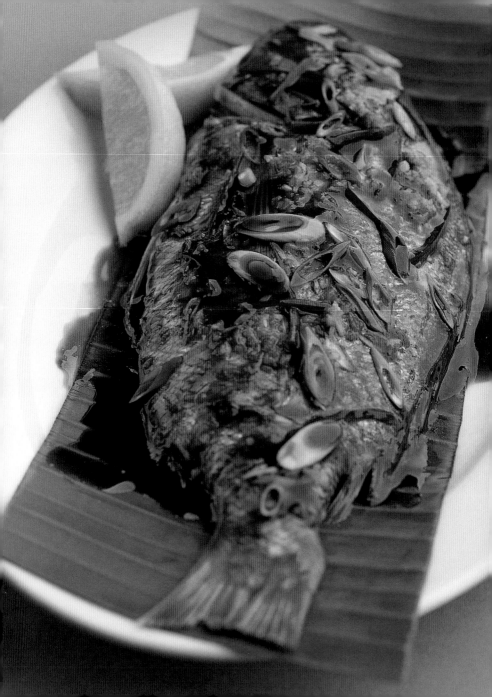

Baked Fish with Spicy Soy Sauce

serves 4

1kg (2lb 3oz) whole snapper

2 teaspoons peanut oil

1 tablespoon lemon juice

pinch of salt

1 lemon, cut into slices

SAUCE

2 teaspoons peanut oil

2 cloves garlic, crushed

2cm (¾in) piece fresh ginger, grated

1 small red chilli, deseeded and sliced

4 spring onions, sliced

2 tablespoons soy sauce

1 tablespoon kecap manis

Preheat oven to 200°C (400°F). Scale, gut and clean the fish (see Introduction) and pat dry. Make 2 diagonal cuts on each side of the fish. Brush fish with oil and lemon juice. Season with salt and place slices of lemon in the fish. Wrap fish up in baking paper and foil and place on a baking tray. Bake in oven for 30–40 minutes or until cooked.

To make the sauce, heat oil in a small saucepan. Add garlic, ginger, chilli and green onions and cook for 1–2 minutes. Add soy sauce, kecap manis and 1/2 cup water and cook for 2–3 minutes.

When fish is cooked, transfer to a large serving dish and pour sauce over. Serve with side bowls of boiled rice.

Roast Sea Bass with Lemon and Basil

serves 4

4 sea bass or bream, about 300g
   (10½oz) each

8 tablespoons olive oil

24 large basil leaves

zest of 1 large lemon

2 tablespoons lemon juice

6 cherry tomatoes, halved

2 teaspoons salt flakes

freshly ground black pepper

Preheat the oven to 220°C (420°F). Scale, gut and clean the fish (see Introduction) and pat dry. Put the olive oil into a large ovenproof dish, add the fish and turn to coat, then tuck 3 basil leaves and a little lemon zest into the belly of each fish. Place the tomatoes in the dish and sprinkle over the remaining basil and lemon zest. Season the fish and tomatoes.

Bake for 20 minutes or until the flesh is firm and cooked through. Sprinkle with lemon juice and serve.

Note Sea bass should not be swamped by strong flavours or a sauce that's too heavy or rich. Lemon and basil are the perfect partners for its delicate taste and texture.

Grilled Sardines

serves 4

12 sardines, cleaned

¼ cup extra virgin olive oil

sea salt

1 lemon, cut into wedges

SALAD

1 green capsicum (bell pepper)

1 yellow capsicum (bell pepper)

3 tomatoes, diced

1 red onion, diced

2 tablespoons extra virgin

olive oil

1 tablespoon white wine vinegar

½ teaspoon sugar

salt and freshly ground black

pepper

Place sardines in a large shallow ceramic dish. Drizzle with olive oil and sprinkle over salt, cover with cling wrap and refrigerate for 1–2 hours.

Preheat a grill or barbecue. Cook sardines for 3–4 minutes each side or until golden and cooked.

To make salad, cut green and yellow capsicum in four and remove seeds.

Place on a baking tray under a hot grill for 6–8 minutes or until skin blisters. Leave to cool, then remove skin and dice. Toss together capsicum, tomatoes, onion, olive oil, vinegar, sugar, salt and pepper.

Serve sardines with lemon wedges and the salad.

Sardines with Spinach and Pine Nuts

serves 4

8 fresh sardines

salt and freshly ground black
   pepper

2 tablespoon olive oil

1 French shallot, finely chopped

1 tablespoon pine nuts

175g (6oz) frozen spinach,
   defrosted and excess moisture
   squeezed out

1 tablespoon sultanas (golden
   raisins)

2 tablespoons fresh breadcrumbs

1 tablespoon lime juice

Preheat the oven to 220°C (420°F). Scale, gut and clean the fish (see Introduction), then cut off the heads. Open out each fish and place skin-side up on the work surface. Press along the length of the backbone with your thumb, then turn the fish over and ease out the backbone, cutting it at the tail end but leaving the tail intact. Rinse and pat dry with absorbent paper, season and turn in 1 tablespoon of the oil.

Heat the remaining oil in a frying pan and fry the shallot and pine nuts for 2–3 minutes until golden. Remove from the heat, then stir in the spinach, sultanas, 1 tablespoon of the breadcrumbs and the lime juice. Season, then use the mixture to sandwich the sardines together in pairs, skin-side out.

Lay the sardines on a baking sheet, sprinkle with the remaining breadcrumbs and bake for 10 minutes or until goldenand cooked through.

Note Fresh sardines are easy to fillet and this fruit, nut and spinach filling will change your view of them forever!

Trout with Almonds and Ginger Sauce

serves 4

salt and freshly ground black
 pepper

4 rainbow trout, cleaned and
 boned

2 tablespoons plain flour

2 tablespoons vegetable oil

90g (3oz) fresh ginger, grated

30g (1oz) butter

90g (3oz) flaked almonds

2 tablespoons currants

Season fish and dust with flour. Heat oil in a large non-stick frying pan over a medium-high heat, add fish and cook for 5 minutes on each side or until crisp, golden and cooked through. Remove from the pan and keep warm.

Squeeze grated ginger over a small bowl to extract the juice—you should have 4–6 teaspoons—and discard the solids.

Add butter and almonds to the frying pan, and cook gently for 2 minutes or until almonds are golden. Add currants and ginger juice, heat through for a few seconds, then spoon over fish and serve immediately.

fillets of fish

Red Snapper with Coconut Sauce

serves 4

600g (1lb 5oz) red snapper

2 stalks lemongrass, very finely sliced

2cm (¾in) piece galangal, grated

6 cloves garlic, roughly chopped

1 French shallot, roughly chopped

2 small red chillies, deseeded

2 kaffir lime leaves

¼ cup dill

1 tablespoon sesame seeds

COCONUT SAUCE

2 cups coconut milk

juice of 2 limes

2 tablespoons palm sugar

1 tablespoon fish sauce

Combine all ingredients except snapper in a food processor and blend to a smooth paste.

Divide fish into four even portions. Remove any major bones. Score skin of fish with a sharp knife.

Smear paste onto snapper, pressing into slits. Set aside for cooking.

Prepare coconut sauce by combining coconut milk, lime juice, palm sugar and fish sauce in a small saucepan. Heat until warm and sugar has dissolved.

Heat a little oil in a frying pan until almost smoking and add fish, skin-side down. Cook until golden brown, about 2 minutes on each side.

Serve with coconut sauce and Asian greens.

Fragrant Salmon Stir-Fry

serves 4

500g (17½oz) skinless wild
   salmon fillets

2 stalks lemongrass

2 tablespoons soy sauce

2cm (¾in) piece fresh ginger,
   grated

2 cloves garlic, crushed

sea salt and freshly ground black
   pepper

¼ cup fresh dill, chopped

¼ cup fresh basil, chopped

1½ tablespoons extra virgin olive
   oil

Cut the salmon into strips about 2.5cm (1in) wide. Peel the outer layer from the lemongrass stalks, then finely chop the lower white bulbous part, discarding the green tops.

Place the lemongrass, soy sauce, ginger, garlic and seasoning in a food processor and process until smooth. Stir through half the dill and half the basil and pulse the processor again for 1–2 seconds.

Arrange the salmon strips in a shallow non-metallic dish and pour the marinade over, turning to coat well. Cover and refrigerate for 2 hours.

Heat 1 tablespoon of the oil in a large, heavy-based frying pan over a medium-high heat, then add the salmon, reserving the marinade. Cook for 2 minutes, then turn and cook for a further 1–2 minutes, until cooked through.

Arrange the salmon on serving plates. Pour the marinade into the frying pan, bring to the boil, then simmer for 2 minutes. Whisk in the remaining oil and season. Spoon the sauce over the salmon and sprinkle the remaining dill and basil over the top.

Fried Fillets with Anchovy Butter

serves 4

4 large plaice or flounder fillets

salt and freshly ground black
   pepper

2 tablespoons plain (all-purpose)
   flour

2 tablespoons vegetable oil or oil
   from the drained anchovies

ANCHOVY BUTTER

50g (1¾oz) canned anchovy fillets
   in olive oil, drained

60g (2oz) unsalted butter,
   softened

1 tablespoon lemon juice

freshly ground black pepper

To make the anchovy butter, blend the anchovies, butter, lemon juice and plenty of pepper until smooth in a food processor, or with a hand blender. Alternatively, mash the anchovies and beat in the other ingredients with a spoon. Shape into a small roll, wrap in baking paper, then place in the refrigerator.

Season the plaice fillets and dust with the flour. Heat 1 tablespoon of oil in a large heavy-based frying pan over a high heat, add 2 plaice fillets, skin-side up, and fry for 1 minute or until golden brown. Turn over and fry for 2 minutes or until browned. Remove from the pan and keep warm. Wipe the pan and cook the remaining fillets in the same way. Unwrap the butter roll and cut into slices, discarding the paper. Serve the fish with green beans, a slice of anchovy butter on top and garnished with chives.

Note The natural saltiness of anchovies goes beautifully with the delicate flavour of the fried plaice.

Lemon and Dill Salmon with Spinach

serves 4

4 salmon fillets, about 250g (9oz) each

1 tablespoon lemon and dill seasoning

salt and freshly ground black pepper

3 tablespoons olive oil

750g (1lb 10oz) desiree potatoes, thinly sliced

1 cup chicken stock

1 bunch English spinach, washed and trimmed

1 lemon, cut into wedges

Place the salmon fillets on a plate and sprinkle both sides evenly with lemon and dill seasoning and pepper. Press lightly to coat.

Heat 1 tablespoon oil in a large frying pan on medium-to-high heat. Add the salmon fillets, skin-side down, and cook for 3 minutes or until the skin is golden and crisp. Turn the fillets and cook for a further 2–3 minutes or until cooked to your liking. Remove and keep warm.

Heat the remaining oil in a large frying pan. Add the potato slices and cook in batches for 1–2 minutes on each side or until just golden. Add the stock, return the remaining potatoes to the pan and simmer for 4–5 minutes or until tender. Add the spinach, season with salt and pepper, and cook until the spinach wilts.

Serve the salmon on a bed of potatoes and spinach with pan juices and lemon wedges.

Note You can vary this dish by using ocean trout fillets or salmon cutlets. The best way to serve salmon is to undercook it a little so it is pink inside. Cooking times for salmon will vary depending on the thickness of the fillet.

Poached Salmon and Citrus Rice

serves 4

1 cup brown rice

zest and juice of 1 lemon

½ cup parsley, finely chopped

4 salmon fillets, about 200g (7oz) each

1 carrot, cut into matchsticks

1 stalk celery, cut into thin strips

1 green capsicum (bell pepper), cut into thin strips

salt and freshly ground black pepper

¼ cup white wine

small bunch dill, roughly chopped

Preheat oven to 200°C (400°F).

Combine the rice with 2 cups water in a saucepan. Bring to the boil, reduce heat to low, cover and cook for 15 minutes. Remove pan from heat, stir through lemon juice and parsley. Stand covered for 10 minutes.

Meanwhile, place the salmon portions on a single sheet of baking paper. Top with lemon zest and finely sliced vegetables, season with salt and pepper and drizzle with white wine. Fold the sides of the baking paper together to form a tight parcel. Bake for 10–12 minutes.

Remove salmon from the parcel, top with baked vegetables and dill. Carefully pour over juices that have collected in the bag. Serve with citrus rice.

Pan-Fried Fish (Ikan Goreng)

serves 4

1 tablespoon peanut oil

4 boneless fish fillets

1 cup coconut milk

1 teaspoon palm sugar or brown
  sugar

1 tablespoon lemon juice

4 green shallots, sliced

PASTE

2 cloves garlic, chopped

2 teaspoons root ginger, chopped

1 stalk lemongrass, sliced

2 medium chillies, deseeded and
  sliced

2 candle nuts

1 teaspoon terasi

1 teaspoon ground coriander

2 teaspoons peanut oil

Grind or pound paste ingredients in a mortar with pestle or a food processor. Brush paste over fish fillets.

Heat remaining oil in a large frying pan. Add fish fillets and cook for 1–2 minutes on each side. Add coconut milk, sugar and lemon juice and simmer for 2–3 minutes. Serve fish topped with green shallots.

Note Macadamia nuts may be substituted for candle nuts.

Teriyaki Fish Fillets

serves 4

4 boneless white fish fillets, about 180g (6oz) each

⅓ cup bought teriyaki marinade (see note)

1 tablespoon lemon juice

1 bunch bok choy, trimmed and separated

TERIYAKI SAUCE

⅓ cup bought teriyaki marinade (see note)

⅓ cup water

½ teaspoon chilli flakes

2 spring onions, sliced

Preheat the oven to 180°C (350°F).

Brush the fish fillets with the marinade. Place on sheets of foil and drizzle each fillet with 1 teaspoon lemon juice. Wrap the fish in foil and place on a baking tray. Bake for 10–15 minutes or until cooked. Remove the fish from the foil and pour any juice from the fish into the sauce.

Boil or steam the bok choy until bright green.

To make the teriyaki sauce, combine all the ingredients and juice from the fish in a small saucepan. Bring to the boil, reduce the heat to low and simmer for 1 minute.

Serve the fish fillets on a bed of steamed bok choy and spoon over teriyaki sauce.

Note If you would prefer to make your own teriyaki marinade, heat all the following ingredients in a pan, stir to combine, then allow to cool: ½ cup soy sauce, 2 tablespoons brown sugar, ½ teaspoon ground ginger, 2 tablespoons white wine vinegar, 1 teaspoon crushed garlic, 2 tablespoons tomato sauce.

Moroccan Seasoned Sardines

serves 4

2½ tablespoons plain (all-purpose) flour

1½ tablespoons Moroccan seasoning

1 teaspoon mint flakes

1 teaspoon dried coriander (cilantro) leaves

salt and freshly ground black pepper

20 sardine fillets

¼ cup olive oil

Combine the flour, Moroccan seasoning, mint, coriander, salt and pepper in a bowl. Coat the sardine fillets in the mixture.

Heat the oil in a frying pan over medium heat. Cook the sardines and crisp.

Serve the sardines with lemon wedges and salad greens.

Note Sardines are best to buy as fillets from your local fish shop. You can vary this recipe by using other seasonings like lemon pepper, Cajun, Creole or Thai. You will need to adjust the seasoning according to taste.

Salmon with Onion and Red Wine

serves 4

½ cup red wine

½ small red onion, finely chopped

75g (2½oz) butter, at room temperature

¼ cup fresh parsley, finely chopped

1 clove garlic, very finely chopped

sea salt and freshly ground black pepper

1 tablespoon sunflower oil

4 salmon fillets, about 175g (6oz) each, skinned

Place the wine and onion in a small saucepan and bring to the boil. Boil rapidly for about 4–5 minutes over a high heat or until reduced to about 2 tablespoons. Remove from the heat and allow to cool completely.

In a bowl, beat the butter until smooth, add the parsley, garlic, seasoning and reduced wine and mix together with a fork. Place the butter in cling wrap on a piece of baking paper and roll up into a tight sausage shape. Refrigerate until hardened.

Heat the oil in a large frying pan over a medium heat and cook the salmon for 4 minutes. Turn and cook for 3–4 minutes more, until cooked through. Cut the butter into four pieces, place one on top of each salmon fillet, and cook for 2 minutes more before serving.

Grilled Salmon Steaks with Mint

serves 4

4 salmon steaks, about 170g (6oz)
each

salt and freshly ground black
pepper

MINT VINAIGRETTE

¼ cup mint, chopped

1 small spring onion, finely
chopped

6 tablespoons olive oil

juice of 1 lemon

Preheat the grill to high and line the grill tray with aluminium foil. Place salmon steaks on top and season lightly. Grill for 4–5 minutes on each side, until lightly browned and cooked through.

To make vinaigrette, mix together mint, shallot, oil and lemon juice, then season to taste. Spoon over salmon steaks and garnish with extra mint.

Fish and Chips with Tartare Sauce

serves 4

90g (3oz) plain (all-purpose) flour

⅓ teaspoon salt

1 tablespoon vegetable oil

4 large potatoes, cut into chunky
    chips

vegetable oil for deep-frying

1 large egg white

4 pieces white fish fillets, about
    170g (6oz) each

TARTARE SAUCE

¾ cup mayonnaise

1 tablespoon capers, drained and
    chopped

1 gherkin, chopped

¼ cup parsley, chopped

1 French shallot, finely chopped

To make sauce, combine mayonnaise, capers, gherkin, parsley and shallot in a bowl. Cover and place in the refrigerator.

Mix flour, salt and oil with ½ cup cold water to make a batter.

Cover chips with cold water, then drain and dry on absorbent paper. Heat oil in a large heavy-based saucepan. Test that oil is ready by adding a potato chip — it should sizzle immediately. Cook chips in 3 or 4 batches for 5–7 minutes each, until golden and cooked. Drain on absorbent paper and keep warm.

Whisk egg white until stiff and fold into the batter. Reduce the heat a little and drop a teaspoon of batter into the oil — it should bubble and firm up straight away. Dip pieces of fish into batter, coating well, then cook for 5–7 minutes, until crisp and golden, then drain on absorbent paper. Sprinkle with salt and serve with chips and tartare sauce.

more seafood ideas

Tuna Seviche

serves 4

500g (17½oz) tuna steaks, diced

½ small red onion, thinly sliced

2 tablespoons extra virgin olive
   oil

⅓ cup lime juice

1 teaspoon Dijon mustard

¼ teaspoon sugar

2 cloves garlic, crushed

1 long red chilli, deseeded and
   finely chopped

salt and freshly ground black
   pepper

1 tablespoon roughly chopped
   roasted peanuts

2 spring onions, sliced

¼ cup coriander (cilantro), freshly
   chopped

Place fish and red onion in a ceramic dish.

Whisk together olive oil, lime juice, Dijon mustard, sugar, garlic and chilli in a jug.

Pour over fish and toss well. Season with salt and pepper.

Cover with cling wrap and refrigerate for 1 hour.

Sprinkle with peanuts, spring onions and coriander and serve with lime wedges.

Turbot with Orange and Tarragon

serves 2

1kg (2lb 3oz) whole turbot
   or firm flesh fish

salt and freshly ground black
   pepper

30g (1oz) butter

SAUCE

30g (1oz) butter

1 French shallot, finely chopped

zest and juice of 1 large orange

⅓ cup dry white wine

¾ cup fish stock

4 sprigs fresh tarragon, leaves
   removed and stalks reserved

juice of 1 lemon

2 teaspoons cornflour
   (cornstarch)

2 tablespoons thickened cream

Preheat the oven to 200°C (400°F).

Scale, gut and clean the fish (see Introduction) and pat dry. Put 5 tablespoons of water into an ovenproof dish the same size as the fish. Season the fish, then place in the dish and dot with butter. Cook for 30 minutes or until the flesh is firm and cooked through.

Meanwhile, make the sauce. Melt the butter in a saucepan and cook the shallot and orange zest for 5 minutes or until softened. Add the wine, stock and tarragon stalks and bring to the boil. Cook briskly for 10 minutes, then strain into a clean pan. Mix the citrus juices with the cornflour, then stir into the sauce and simmer for 2–3 minutes, until slightly thickened. Remove from the heat and stir in the cream and tarragon leaves, then season.

Cut the fish from head to tail, along the backbone, cutting to the bone. Remove the skin, then lift off the 2 fillets with a knife. Remove the bone to reveal the remaining 2 fillets. Serve with the sauce.

Note Turbot is expensive, but worth it. The orange and tarragon sauce makes the most of its flavour. Serve with sugar snap peas and julienned carrots.

Tuna al Forno

serves 4

1 cup long-grain rice

1 tablespoon olive oil

½ large onion, finely diced

1 clove garlic, crushed

1 cup thickened cream

1 cup tomato pasta sauce

½ cup semi-dried tomatoes, chopped

185g (6½oz) canned tuna

4 spring onions, chopped

¼ cup basil, finely chopped

50g (1¾oz) provolone cheese, diced, plus 100g (3½oz) grated

salt and freshly ground black pepper

Preheat oven to 200°C (400°F).

Combine the rice with 2 cups water in a saucepan. Bring to the boil, reduce heat to low, cover and cook for 15 minutes. Remove from heat, allow to stand covered for 10 minutes.

Heat oil in a large pan over high heat. Add onion and garlic and cook gently for 2–3 minutes or until softened. Add cream, pasta sauce and semi-dried tomatoes, toss well to combine.

Line a well-oiled baking dish with cooked rice. Scatter with tuna, spring onion, basil and diced cheese, season, then pour over sauce. Top with grated cheese. Bake for 20 minutes or until cheese has melted and browned.

Spanish-Style Fish Cutlets

serves 4

4 jewfish cutlets

3 tablespoons olive oil

¼ cup parsley, finely chopped

3 large cloves garlic, crushed

2 tablespoons slivered almonds

1 spring onion, chopped

½ teaspoon ground paprika

zest of ½ lemon

400g (14oz) canned chopped
   tomatoes, drained

Preheat oven to 180°C (350°F). Arrange fish in a shallow ovenproof dish lightly brushed with olive oil. Brush the top of each cutlet with half the olive oil.

Combine parsley, garlic, almonds, spring onion, paprika, lemon zest and remaining olive oil. Spoon over fish and press down well.

Bake for 10 minutes. Pour the tomatoes around the fish and cook for a further 10 minutes or until fish is cooked.

Swordfish with Lime and Herb Butter

serves 4

1 tablespoon vegetable oil

juice of 1 lime

salt and freshly ground black
   pepper

4 swordfish steaks, about 170g
   (6oz) each

LIME AND HERB BUTTER

60g (2oz) butter, softened

finely grated zest and juice of 1
   lime

¼ cup coriander (cilantro) leaves,
   chopped

salt and freshly ground black
   pepper

Mix together the oil, lime juice and seasoning in a shallow non-metallic bowl. Add the fish steaks and turn to coat.

Cover and refrigerate for at least 15 minutes, or up to 8 hours.

To make the lime and herb butter, beat the butter until smooth, then slowly beat in the lime zest and juice and the coriander. Season, then shape into a small roll, wrap in baking paper and refrigerate.

Preheat the grill to high. Cook the swordfish close to the heat source for 4 minutes on each side, until lightly browned and cooked through. Unwrap the butter and cut into slices, discarding the paper.

Serve the fish on couscous, topped with a slice of butter and garnished with extra coriander.

Tuna and Broccoli Pies

serves 4

1 small onion, chopped

30g (1oz) butter

1 tablespoon plain flour

⅔ cup milk

50g (1¾oz) Cheddar cheese, grated

½ head broccoli, cut into florets and blanched

185g (6½oz) canned tuna, drained

1 large sheet shortcrust pastry

1 standard sheet puff pastry

1 egg, lightly beaten with dash of milk

Sauté onion in butter for 2–3 minutes. Add flour and stir well, then whisk in milk and Cheddar until smooth. Combine with broccoli and tuna and mix well.

Preheat oven to 200°C (400°F), or preheat an electric pie maker. Using a pastry cutter 12cm in diameter, cut 4 rounds out of the shortcrust pastry. Cut five 2cm-long (¾in) incisions into the sides of the pastry rounds. Using a 10cm (4in) pastry cutter, cut 4 rounds out of the puff pastry.

Place shortcrust pastry rounds into large muffin tin moulds, making sure that the pastry slightly overlaps where the incisions have been made. If using an electric pie maker, place pastry in the moulds. Divide filling evenly between each pie case.

If using the oven, top each pie with a puff pastry round. Using your fingers, crimp edges of both pastries together to make a seal. Brush with egg wash and bake for 15–20 minutes.

If using an electric pie maker, top each pie with a puff pastry round. Brush with egg wash and close. Cook for 8–10 minutes.

Tuna and Caper Vol-Au-Vents

serves 4

50g (1¾oz) butter

4 spring onions, sliced

⅓ cup plain (all-purpose) flour

2 cups milk

2 teaspoons lemon and dill
   seasoning

¼ cup lemon juice

425g (15oz) canned tuna, drained
   and flaked

2 tablespoons capers, drained

¼ small bunch chives, chopped

8 large vol-au-vent pastry cases

Preheat the oven to 180°C (350°F).

Heat the butter in a saucepan. Add the spring onions and cook for 1–2 minutes. Add the flour and cook for 1 minute. Add the milk slowly, stirring until the mixture boils and is smooth. Add the lemon and dill seasoning, lemon juice, tuna, capers and chives. Stir until the mixture thickens and is smooth. Add a little extra milk if mixture is too thick.

Place the vol-au-vent cases on a baking tray and bake for 8–10 minutes or until crisp. Spoon the mixture into the cases and serve immediately. Garnish with extra chives. Serve with crusty bread as an entrée or as a light meal with salad greens.

Note There are quite a few different size vol-au-vent cases available—use the small cocktail size for parties. You can also substitute salmon for tuna.

Tuna and Spring Onion Fish Cakes

serves 4

4 slices bread, crusts removed

700g (1lb 8oz) floury potatoes, halved or quartered depending on size

3 tablespoons mayonnaise

400g (14oz) canned tuna in oil, drained and flaked

¼ cup parsley, chopped

2 spring onions, finely chopped

finely grated zest of 1 small lemon

3 tablespoons plain flour

1 medium egg, beaten

vegetable oil for frying

Preheat the oven to 160°C (325°F). Place the bread on a baking sheet and cook at the bottom of the oven for 20–30 minutes until crisp. Cool, break into pieces and crush with a rolling pin.

Meanwhile, cook the potatoes in a large saucepan of boiling salted water for 15 minutes or until tender. Drain, transfer to a bowl and mash with the mayonnaise. Leave to cool for 30 minutes.

Mash the tuna, parsley, spring onions and lemon zest into the potatoes. Flour your hands, then shape the mixture into 8 flat cakes. Dust with flour and dip into the egg, then into the breadcrumbs.

Heat 5mm (1/8in) of oil in a large heavy-based frying pan and cook the fish cakes for 3–4 minutes on each side until crisp and golden (you may have to cook them in batches). Drain on absorbent paper, then serve with the lemon wedges.

Note These chunky fish cakes are packed with flavour and it only takes a few vegetables or a salad to make a complete meal. Canned salmon works just as well as the tuna.

Tuna Niçoise

serves 8

170g (6oz) green beans, cut into 8cm (3⅛in) lengths

4 tablespoons olive oil

4 tuna steaks, about 170g (6oz) each and 2.5cm (1in) thick

salt and freshly ground black pepper

1 red capsicum (bell pepper), deseeded and diced

12 cherry tomatoes, halved

16 black olives, pitted

1 tablespoon balsamic vinegar

¼ cup flat-leaf parsley

Cook beans in boiling salted water for 3–5 minutes, until tender but still firm to the bite. Drain, refresh under cold water and set aside. Place 2 tablespoons of oil in a shallow bowl, add tuna and turn to coat, then season lightly.

Heat a large heavy-based frying pan over a high heat, then add tuna and cook for 1 minute on each side. Reduce the heat and cook for a further 1–2 minutes on each side, until steaks have browned slightly. Set aside.

Heat remaining oil in the frying pan and fry the red capsicum for 1 minute or until softened. Add the beans, tomatoes and olives and stir-fry for 1 minute to warm through. Remove from the pan, pour in vinegar, and use it to deglaze the pan. Serve tuna topped with the capsicum mixture and parsley, then drizzle the vinegar mixture.

Barbecued Seafood Salad

serves 8

2 tablespoons lemon juice

1 tablespoon olive oil

300g (10½oz) firm white fish
  swordfish, mackerel or cod, cut
  into 21 2cm (¾in) cubes

300g (10½oz) pink fish (salmon,
  ocean trout, marlin or tuna)

12 scallops

12 uncooked prawns (shrimp)
  (with or without shell)

1 calamari (squid), cleaned and
  tube cut into rings

1 large onion, cut into rings

1 telegraph cucumber, sliced

1 bunch watercress

RASPBERRY AND TARRAGON
  DRESSING

3 tablespoons fresh tarragon

2 tablespoons wine vinegar

2 tablespoons lemon juice

1 tablespoon olive oil

freshly ground black pepper

Place lemon juice and oil in a bowl. Whisk to combine. Add white and pink fish, scallops, prawns (shrimp) and calamari. Toss to combine. Cover. Marinate in the refrigerator for 1 hour or until ready to use. Do not marinate for longer than 2 hours.

Preheat a barbecue or char-grill pan until very hot. Drain seafood mixture and place on barbecue hotplate or in pan. Add onion. Cook, turning several times, for 6–8 minutes or until seafood is just cooked. Take care not to overcook or the seafood will be tough and dry. Transfer cooked seafood to a bowl and cool, then add cucumber.

Line a serving platter with watercress, and arrange seafood and cucumber on top.

To make dressing, place tarragon, vinegar, lemon juice, oil and black pepper to taste in a screwtop jar. Shake to combine.

Drizzle dressing over salad, and serve immediately.

Index

UK £9.99
USA $14.99